Dear Parent:
Your child's love of readi

GW00994518

Every child learns to read in a different w
You can help your young reader improve
by encouraging his or her own interests and abilities. You can also guide
your child's spiritual development by reading stories with biblical values
and Bible stories, like I Can Read! books published by Zonderkidz. From
books your child reads with you to the first books he or she reads alone,
there are I Can Read! books for every stage of reading:

SHARED READING
Basic language, word repetition, and whimsical
illustrations, ideal for sharing with your emergent reader.

BEGINNING READING
Short sentences, familiar words, and simple concepts for
children eager to read on their own.

READING WITH HELP
Engaging stories, longer sentences, and language play
for developing readers.

READING ALONE
Complex plots, challenging vocabulary, and high-interest
topics for the independent reader.

ADVANCED READING
Short paragraphs, chapters, and exciting themes for the
perfect bridge to chapter books.

I Can Read! books have introduced children to the joy of reading since
1957. Featuring award-winning authors and illustrators and a fabulous
cast of beloved characters, I Can Read! books set the standard for
beginning readers.

A lifetime of discovery begins with the magical words "I Can Read!"

Visit www.icanread.com for information on enriching your child's reading experience.
Visit www.zonderkidz.com for more Zonderkidz I Can Read! titles.

How many are your works, LORD!
In wisdom you made them all;
the earth is full of your creatures.
—*Psalm 104:24*

ZONDERKIDZ

Forest Friends
Copyright © 2011 by Zonderkidz

Requests for information should be addressed to:
Zonderkidz, *Grand Rapids, Michigan 49530*

Library of Congress Cataloging-in-Publication Data

Forest friends.
   p. cm.
  ISBN 978-0-310-72190-1 (softcover)
  1. Forest animals—Religious aspects—Christianity—Juvenile literature. 2. Creation—Juvenile literature.
  BT746.F67 2010
  231.7–dc22   2010037919

Editor: Mary Hassinger
Art direction: Jody Langley

Printed in China
11 12 13 14 15 16 17 /SCC/ 10 9 8 7 6 5 4 3 2 1

···MADE·BY·GOD···

Forest Friends

CONTENTS

God created everything

and made it all good.

He made beautiful forests filled

with animals.

The forest has some small animals

and some really big ones too!

One really big forest animal is the …

MOOSE!

Moose are large mammals.

Some are seven feet tall!

That does not include their antlers.

One of the biggest racks of antlers

was over six feet wide!

Male moose are called bulls.

Female moose are called cows.

Baby moose are called calves.

Moose have long legs
that help them run fast.
They can trot at a speed
of 35 miles an hour.

Moose are very good swimmers.

They can stay underwater

for up to a minute.

Some can dive 20 feet underwater.

Do you know another forest animal

that is a good swimmer?

It is the …

PORCUPINE!

Porcupines' backs are covered with long, needle-like spines called quills.
These quills are hollow.
The quills help them float.

Be careful around porcupines!

Their quills can grow up to a foot long.

They are very, very sharp.

Porcupines are born with soft bristles.

The bristles harden with time.

Besides being good swimmers,
porcupines can climb!
Some can climb 100 feet up trees
where they eat branches and leaves.
They also eat fruit and tender leaf and
flower buds.

There are 24 kinds of porcupines.

They live in North and South America,

Europe, Asia, and Africa.

Porcupines live on the ground in forests,

deserts, and grasslands.

Babies are called porcupettes.

Porcupines are actually large rodents.

They are related to mice and gerbils.

Porcupines are nocturnal
like many rodents.
This means they are awake at night
and sleep during the day.

You might recognize

another nocturnal animal

by the rings on its tail.

They are sometimes called burglars

because it looks like they wear masks.

It is a …

RACCOON!

Raccoon babies are called cubs or kits
and are actually born without
the black "mask."
They are curious and sneaky.
Many people see raccoons sneaking in
their garbage, gardens, or yards.

Raccoons like to eat almost anything!

Their favorite foods are frogs,

mice, bugs, eggs, fruit, and garbage.

They use their paws like little hands,

holding their food just like a person.

Raccoons live in safe places
like hollow logs, caves, or small
shelters, but they like warm, dry places
like chimneys too!
You can see raccoons in the forest but
they like to be in neighborhoods.

God made moose huge, raccoons curious,

and porcupines prickly.

He made another animal in the forest

that is very sly.

It is called a …

FOX!

Foxes are related to dogs,

but sometimes they act more like cats.

Foxes stalk their prey and play with it.

And just like a cat, they use

their tails for balance.

There are many breeds of foxes.

Some live in the forest

and are sandy, red, silver, or even black.

This breed is called the red fox.

Fox hunt for a lot of their food.

They eat many things such as mice,

frogs, insects, birds, and rabbits.

They also like fruits and vegetables.

Male foxes are called dog foxes.
Female foxes are called vixen, and
babies are cubs.

Just like many forest animals,
foxes have become used to people
and can be found in neighborhoods
as well as the woods where
they normally live.

God created everything.

From the giant moose to the clever fox,

and everything in between!

The forest and our whole world

is filled with God's great creation!